Personal Hygiene?
What's that Got to Do with Me?

of related interest

Help for the Child with Asperger's Syndrome
A Parent's Guide to Negotiating the Social Service Maze
Gretchen Mertz
Foreword by Tony Attwood
ISBN 1 84310 780 5

Succeeding in College with Asperger Syndrome
A student guide
John Harpur, Maria Lawlor and Michael Fitzgerald
ISBN 1 84310 201 3

Asperger's Syndrome
A Guide for Parents and Professionals
Tony Attwood
Foreword by Lorna Wing
ISBN 1 85302 577 1

Freaks, Geeks and Asperger Syndrome
A User Guide to Adolescence
Luke Jackson
Foreword by Tony Attwood
ISBN 1 84310 098 3
Winner of the NASEN & TES Special Educational Needs Children's Book Award 2003

Asperger Syndrome in Adolescence
Living with the Ups, the Downs and Things in Between
Edited by Liane Holliday Willey
Foreword by Luke Jackson
ISBN 1 84310 742 2

Asperger Syndrome, Adolescence, and Identity
Looking Beyond the Label
Harvey Molloy and Latika Vasil
ISBN 1 84310 126 2

Personal Hygiene? What's that Got to Do with Me?

Pat Crissey

Illustrated by Noah Crissey

Jessica Kingsley Publishers
London and Philadelphia

Cover artwork by Noah Crissey

First published in 2005
by Jessica Kingsley Publishers
116 Pentonville Road
London N1 9JB, UK
and
400 Market Street, Suite 400
Philadelphia, PA 19106, USA

www.jkp.com

Copyright © Pat Crissey 2005
Illustrations copyright © Noah Crissey 2005
Second impression 2005
Third impression 2006

Library of Congress Cataloging in Publication Data
Crissey, Pat, 1946-
    Personal hygiene? What's that got to do with me? / Pat Crissey ;
illustrated by Noah Crissey.
        p. cm.
    ISBN-13: 978-1-84310-796-5 (pbk.)
    ISBN-10: 1-84310-796-1 (pbk.)
    1. Autistic children—Health and hygiene—Juvenile literature.
    2. Asperger's syndrome—Patients—Health and hygiene—Juvenile
literature.   I. Crissey, Noah. II. Title. III. Title: Personal
hygiene?
    RJ506.A9C75 2005
    649'.154—dc22

                                                                2004024966

British Library Cataloguing in Publication Data
A CIP catalogue record for this book is available from the British Library

ISBN-13: 978 1 84310 796 5
ISBN-10: 1 84310 796 1

Printed and Bound in Great Britain by
Athenaeum Press, Gateshead, Tyne and Wear

Contents

Contents

Introduction: What is Personal Hygiene?

Words to know:

Hygiene – the practice of staying healthy and preventing disease by keeping yourself clean

Deodorant – a substance that is put on the skin under the arms which covers up body odor

Employer – someone who hires people to do work for money

Employee – a person who works for someone else and gets paid money to do it

Personal hygiene is all the things we do to keep our bodies clean and healthy. Keeping your body clean includes not only bathing and washing your hands, but also taking care of your hair and your teeth, keeping your fingernails clean and trimmed, and making sure to put on deodorant and wear clean clothes. It's a lot to remember, but it makes a huge difference to what other people think about you. When someone has good personal hygiene, they look good, they smell good, and they feel good. Other people like to be around them.

When someone does not have good hygiene, they look dirty and they smell bad. Other kids at school won't want to hang out with someone who is dirty or smells bad. On the job, an employer won't want to hire someone who has poor hygiene. Other workers won't want to work with someone who isn't clean. Another important reason to have good personal hygiene is so that you will stay healthy. When you keep yourself clean, you won't get sick as often.

So, follow along while we show you what you can do to look good, smell good, and feel good.

Look good   **Smell good**   **Feel good**

? Questions

✓ **Tick all answers that are correct.**

1. Which of the following are part of personal hygiene?

   ☐ Taking a bath or shower

   ☐ Playing video games

   ☐ Washing your hands

   ☐ Shampooing your hair

   ☐ Brushing your teeth

   ☐ Feeding the cat

2. Why is personal hygiene important?

   ☐ So you will look and smell clean

   ☐ So other people will like to be around you

   ☐ To help you stay healthy

   ☐ Because breakfast is the most important meal of the day

   ☐ Employers don't like to hire employees who look dirty

1. Looking Clean, Smelling Clean

Words to know:

Antiperspirant – a substance that is put on the skin to prevent perspiration

Armpit – the hollow area under the arm at the shoulder

Bacteria – tiny living things that can be seen only through a microscope. Bacteria are everywhere. Some bacteria are very useful and other bacteria cause people to get sick

Deodorant – a substance that is put on the skin under the arms which covers up body odor

Groin – the part of the body between the two legs

Perspiration – a salty liquid that comes through the pores of the skin; another word for sweat

Pore – a tiny opening in the skin. Perspiration passes through the pores of the skin

---

When we become teenagers our bodies change. Our sweat glands become more active and we sweat more. We sweat when we are hot and when we are nervous. Sometimes people sweat a lot and sometimes just a little. But people are always sweating, even when they don't feel hot.

Perspiration is another name for sweat. When perspiration comes out of our pores, it has no smell. But within seconds, bacteria that are on our bodies or in the air will begin to live and grow in the perspiration and soon our sweat starts to smell bad. Often we cannot smell our own sweat because the odor starts to grow slowly and our nose gets used to it and we don't notice it. But other people smell it and think it smells bad. Sometimes people call this smell B.O. That stands for body odor.

The best way to keep from smelling bad is to take a bath or shower every day using warm water and soap. When we bathe, the bacteria get washed away. If we don't wash off the bacteria every day, more and more bacteria will start growing on our skin and the smell gets worse and worse. It's especially important to wash the armpits and groin area well, because these parts of the body provide a perfect place for bacteria to grow.

Putting deodorant or antiperspirant on every day, after a bath or shower, also helps keep us smelling good. A deodorant is a good-smelling substance that is put on the skin under the arms to cover up body odor. An antiperspirant is a substance that actually prevents perspiration. Most people use the word deodorant to mean both deodorants and antiperspirants. When you go to the store to buy deodorant, if you look on the label it will probably say "Antiperspirant & Deodorant." This means it prevents perspiration and it has a good smell which will help cover up the smell of B.O. Deodorants come in sticks, roll-ons, or sprays and are available at any drugstore or supermarket.

If we put deodorant on without first washing away the bacteria, the bacteria from the day before are still there and will continue to grow. The deodorant will cover up the smell for a short while, but in a few hours the smell will get worse.

As well as using deodorant, it is also important to put on clean clothes every day. Once clothes have been worn they have sweat and bacteria on them. They can look clean, but they will start smelling as the bacteria start growing.

If we don't keep ourselves clean, the bacteria in our sweat will grow and smell bad. Other people will think we smell bad. Most people do not like to be around people who smell bad.

It is important to keep ourselves clean. If we are clean we will feel better and stay healthier. If we take a bath or shower every day, use deodorant, and wear clean clothes, we will smell good. Other people like being around people who smell good.

To look, smell, and feel clean:

| **1. Bathe every day** | **2. Put on deodorant** | **3. Put on clean clothes** |

? Questions

✓ Tick all answers that are correct.

1. What causes perspiration to smell bad?

    ☐ Salt from your skin

    ☐ The bacteria growing in it

    ☐ Onions

2. What can you do to get rid of bacteria on your skin?

    ☐ Take a bath or shower every day using warm water and soap

    ☐ Brush it off with your hand

    ☐ Put deodorant on

3. What will happen if you put deodorant on without bathing first?

    ☐ The bacteria on the skin will continue to grow and after a short while you will smell bad

    ☐ It will make you smell good all day

    ☐ It could make your feet hurt

4. Why is it important to always put clean clothes on after a bath or shower?

    ☐ So that there are lots of dirty clothes to be washed

    ☐ Because the clothes you've worn have sweat and bacteria on them and can smell bad

    ☐ So you look neat and clean

5.   When should you put deodorant on?

    ☐ Every day after your bath or shower

    ☐ When you feel hot

    ☐ Before you take a shower

List the 3 steps to smelling and feeling clean.

1. _____

2. _____

3. _____

2. Turning Bad Hair Days into Good Hair Days

Words to know:

Bacteria – tiny living things that can be seen only through a microscope. Bacteria are everywhere. Some bacteria are very useful and other bacteria cause people to get sick

Dandruff – a skin condition of the scalp that produces small white flakes of dried skin

Gland – a small organ of the body that makes substances. Sweat glands make sweat to control the body's temperature

Perspiration – a salty liquid that comes through the pores of the skin; another word for sweat

Another change teenagers notice is to their hair. Each single hair has its own oil gland, which keeps the hair shiny and healthy. During the teenage years, these glands produce extra oil, which can make the hair look too oily or greasy. This makes it harder to keep your hair looking clean.

Hair that isn't clean will look oily and can smell bad too. Hair starts smelling bad because of the bacteria and perspiration on it. As the bacteria grow they start to stink, just like the bacteria on your skin do.

To keep your hair looking and smelling clean, shampoo it every day when you take a bath or shower. When you shampoo your hair, bacteria get washed away.

Use enough shampoo to work up a good lather, but not too much. Squeeze enough shampoo into your hand to make a small circle. If you don't use enough shampoo, your hair won't get clean. If you use too much, it will be hard to rinse it all away. It's important to rinse your hair until all the shampoo is gone, or your hair can look sticky and dirty.

Some people have dandruff. Dandruff happens when the oil from the glands on your head mixes with dead skin and dirt from the air. Then it breaks off in small clumps and leaves little white specks in your hair and on your clothes. To get rid of dandruff, shampoo your hair every day. There are special dandruff shampoos that can be used.

Afterwards, it's important to remember to comb your hair, unless your hair is very short. Hair that has not been combed looks messy. Sometimes people will say messy hair looks like a rat's nest.

One of the first things that people notice about you is your hair. People don't like to look at hair that is dirty or messy. People don't like to smell hair that smells bad. When your hair is dirty or messy, you are having a bad hair day.

To have a good hair day:

1. Shampoo hair every day

2. Comb hair

3. Look great!

? Questions

✓ Tick all answers that are correct.

1. What will happen if you don't shampoo your hair regularly?

   ☐ Your hair will look oily

   ☐ Your feet will sweat

   ☐ Your hair will look messy

   ☐ Your hair will smell bad

2. What makes hair smell bad?

   ☐ Shampoo

   ☐ The bacteria and perspiration on your head

   ☐ Dandruff

3. What can you do to get rid of dandruff?

   ☐ Use deodorant every day

   ☐ Shampoo your hair every day

   ☐ Use a dandruff shampoo

List the 2 steps to having a good hair day.

1. _____

2. _____

3. Clean Teeth, Great Smile

Words to know:

Bacteria – tiny living things that can be seen only through a microscope. Bacteria are everywhere. Some bacteria are very useful and other bacteria cause people to get sick

Cavity – a hole in a tooth, caused by decay

Floss – sliding a piece of thin coated string, called dental floss, up and down between your teeth

Keeping your teeth clean is important for several reasons. One is that brushing and flossing your teeth gets rid of the bacteria in your mouth that cause cavities and gum disease. Cavities and gum disease cause pain and need to be taken care of by a dentist. Brushing regularly is the best way to keep your teeth healthy.

Another reason for keeping your teeth clean is that your teeth look nice and you look good when you smile. When you don't brush your teeth, food particles stick to your teeth and your teeth look yellow and dirty. Brushing your teeth is also important so that you don't have bad breath.

When brushing your teeth remember the following:

- Use a soft toothbrush and replace it when it's worn.

- Brush at least twice a day – in the morning after breakfast and before going to bed.

- Brush all of your teeth, not just the ones at the front.

- Brush all sides of your teeth, insides, outsides, and on top.

- Brush away from your gums.

- Take your time. Brush your teeth for 2 minutes.

- Then brush your tongue a few times.

It's also really important to floss your teeth because food particles and bacteria get stuck between your teeth. It's impossible for a toothbrush to reach between your teeth to remove these particles and bacteria. Flossing helps keep your teeth clean and prevents gum disease.

When flossing remember the following:

- Use a piece of floss about 18 inches long, and wrap it around your fingers like in the picture.

- Gently push the floss between your teeth and rub both sides up and down. Floss between all your teeth.

- Floss once every day.

To keep your teeth clean and healthy:

1. Brush your teeth every morning

2. Brush your teeth every night

3. Floss once a day

❓ Questions

✓ Tick all answers that are correct.

1. Why is it important to brush your teeth regularly?

   ☐ So you don't get cavities

   ☐ So you don't have bad breath

   ☐ So your teeth look good

   ☐ So you don't have body odor

2. How often do you need to brush your teeth?

   ☐ Once a day

   ☐ Every morning when you get up and every night before bed

   ☐ Once a week

   ☐ Every hour

3. When brushing your teeth, how long should you actually brush?

   ☐ 2 minutes

   ☐ 2 seconds

   ☐ 1 minute

   ☐ 2 hours

4. Why do you need to floss?

□ To remove pieces of food that get caught between the teeth

□ You only need to floss if you don't brush your teeth

□ Flossing keeps your gums healthy

□ You usually cannot feel the bacteria and food stuck between your teeth

5. How often do you need to floss?

□ Once a day

□ Twice a day

□ Once a week

□ Only on your birthday

List the 3 steps for clean and healthy teeth.

1. _____

2. _____

3. _____

4. Taming Dragon Breath

> **Words to know:**
>
> **Bacteria** – tiny living things that can be seen only through a microscope. Bacteria are everywhere. Some bacteria are very useful and other bacteria cause people to get sick

Bad breath is usually caused by bacteria growing in the mouth. The inside of your mouth is the perfect place for bacteria to live and grow. It is dark, wet and warm. Odor-causing bacteria can grow and cause bad breath. This is especially true overnight. While you are sleeping, bacteria in your mouth are growing quickly, and that is why when most people wake up in the morning their breath smells bad. People often call this "morning breath." Other terms used to describe bad breath are "dog breath" and "dragon breath."

You usually cannot tell when you have bad breath. Your nose becomes accustomed to the smell of your breath and you don't notice that your breath smells bad. But other people do notice and find the smell unpleasant. Sometimes people will turn away or back away when someone who has bad breath is talking to them.

There are things you can do to make your breath smell good. First you need to be sure to brush your teeth at least twice a day, morning and night. It helps if you take your toothbrush and brush your tongue as well. Bacteria hide in the cracks of the tongue and you need to brush your tongue to get rid of it.

For good-smelling breath:

1. Brush your teeth every morning

2. Brush your teeth every night

3. Brush your tongue

❓ Questions

✓ Tick all answers that are correct.

1. Why do people have "morning breath"?

   ☐ Because they ate candy the night before

   ☐ Because they didn't floss before going to bed

   ☐ Because bacteria grow in the mouth all night

2. How do you get rid of bacteria that live in the cracks of your tongue?

   ☐ Scrape them off with a spoon

   ☐ Brush your tongue with your toothbrush when you brush your teeth

   ☐ Floss your teeth once a day

3. Which of the following are true?

   ☐ Most people's breath smells bad first thing in the morning

   ☐ You usually can't tell when you have bad breath

   ☐ You can smell it when your own breath smells bad

List the 3 steps to take to have good smelling breath.

1. _____

2. _____

3. _____

5. Having a Hand People Want to Shake

Words to know:

Germs – tiny living things that cause disease

Jagged – rough, with sharp edges

Nail brush – a small brush used for scrubbing under fingernails

Nail clippers – a small tool used to clip fingernails and toenails

Nail file – a small flat file used for shaping fingernails

Frequent, thorough hand washing is one of the most important things you can do to stay healthy and to look clean. Germs are everywhere, even though they are so small you can't see them. While some germs are harmless, other germs cause the flu, colds, and other illnesses. We are constantly getting germs on our hands from touching objects that other people have touched, such as door knobs, handles, stair railings, etc. We can also get germs from touching surfaces that people have sneezed or coughed on.

When we forget to wash our hands, these germs get into our bodies when we touch food that we eat, or touch our eyes, nose or mouth. Once the germs are inside your body, they can grow and make you sick.

Thorough hand washing with warm water and soap gets rid of most of the germs on our hands and is the best way to prevent illness. Lots of germs hide between the fingers and under the fingernails, so it is especially important to scrub those areas.

Because we are constantly using our hands in everything we do, other people notice our hands. When people see hands that look dirty, with dirt under the fingernails, they think it looks gross. People don't want to shake hands with someone with dirty hands because they think all that dirt and germs will get on them.

To stay healthy and keep your hands looking clean you need to wash your hands:

- ○ Before preparing, touching, or eating food
- ○ After using the toilet
- ○ After blowing your nose, petting or handling an animal, or handling garbage or anything that is dirty.

To wash your hands thoroughly, you need to:

- ○ Use warm running water and soap.
- ○ Rub hands together for at least 10 seconds.
- ○ Rub between the fingers.
- ○ Scrub under the fingernails.

○ Rinse thoroughly and dry with a paper towel, a clean cloth towel, or a hand dryer.

It's also important to keep your nails looking clean and groomed. Dirty jagged nails look bad and can catch on clothes or hair. A nail brush can be used to scrub nails, and if they still aren't clean use a nail file to clean dirt out from under the nail. Most boys use nail clippers to keep their nails short. Girls will often let their nails grow a little longer, but will use a nail file to keep them rounded and smooth.

To keep your hands clean and looking good:

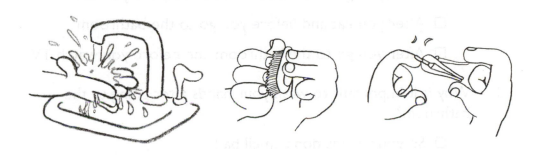

| **1. Wash your hands often** | **2. Clean fingernails** | **3. Trim fingernails** |

? Questions

✓ Tick all answers that are correct.

1. Why is it important to wash your hands often?

    ☐ So your hands don't look dirty and gross

    ☐ To get rid of germs that could make you sick

    ☐ So people will want to shake your hand

    ☐ So your breath doesn't smell bad

2. When are the two most important times to wash your hands?

    ☐ After you go to the bathroom and before you eat

    ☐ After you eat and before you go to the bathroom

    ☐ After you go to the bathroom and before you watch TV

3. Why is it important to wash your hands after going to the bathroom?

    ☐ So your hands don't smell bad

    ☐ So you don't get germs from the bathroom on things you touch, like food

    ☐ To wash away any germs that might have gotten on your hands when you went to the bathroom

    ☐ To keep the sink clean

4. Why is it important to clean your fingernails?

    ☐ So your nails will grow faster

    ☐ Because germs can hide under the fingernails

    ☐ Because dirty nails look gross

5.   What do you need to do to keep nails from looking jagged?

☐ Use a nail clipper or nail file to trim or shape your nails

☐ Rub your nails with a towel

☐ Chew on your nails to get them even

List the 3 steps to having good-looking hands.

1. _____

2. _____

3. _____

6. There's Hair Everywhere!

Words to know:

Optional – something that you don't have to do. It's your choice whether you want to or not

Mustache – the hair growing on the upper lip

Razor – a sharp-edged instrument used to shave hair on the face, underarms, or legs

Boys

Another way our bodies change when we become teenagers is that hair starts growing where it didn't grow before. Boys will start noticing hair growing in lots of unusual places, like in the armpits, in the groin area, and on the face. The only thing that needs to be done about hair that grows in the armpits and groin area is to make sure that you wash those areas well, using soap, to get rid of odor. Hair makes it easier for bacteria and sweat to hide there.

Once you start noticing hair growing on your face, you'll probably want to start shaving. Shaving is optional because some men like to grow a mustache or beard. But when hair first starts growing on your face, there won't be that much of it, so if you let it grow it won't look like a real mustache or beard. It will just make you look sloppy, like you just got out of bed. So, most boys shave the hair on their face so that they can look neat and clean.

The best way to shave the hair on your face is to use an electric razor. Electric razors are made so that they can't cut you and are therefore a lot safer than regular razors. Some electric razors use batteries and don't need to be plugged into an outlet. Others have a cord that you plug in.

The best time to shave is in the morning so that you will look neat and clean when you get to school or work. You might also want to shave before you go out if you go somewhere in the evening. Make sure you watch carefully in a mirror while you are shaving to make sure you don't miss any areas. It looks pretty bad when part of your face is clean shaven and part of it is hairy.

When people say someone is "clean shaven" that means they think he looks good. They think he looks neat and clean and it looks like he just shaved. When they say that someone has a five o'clock shadow, it means it looks like he hasn't shaved for a while. You can see the little hairs growing back on his face, as you often can around 5:00p.m. when someone shaved early in the morning.

For that clean-shaven look:

1. Shave every morning

2. Look clean shaven

? Questions

✓ **Tick all answers that are correct.**

1. Once you have hair growing on your face, how often do you need to shave?

   ☐ At least once a day

   ☐ Every half hour

   ☐ Once a week

   ☐ When the hair on your face is 1/2 inch long

2. Why is it important to look in a mirror while you are shaving?

   ☐ Otherwise the razor won't work

   ☐ So you can see what you're doing

   ☐ If you don't you can miss areas and have spots that are hairy

List the two things you need to do to look clean shaven.

1. _____

2. _____

Girls

During the teenage years, girls will start noticing hair growing all kinds of places where it didn't grow before, like in their armpits, in the groin area, and on their legs. Some girls don't like to have hairy pits (hair growing in the armpits) or long, dark hairs growing on their legs.

One thing you can do to get rid of unwanted hair in your armpits and on your legs is to shave. The best time to shave is right after your shower or bath. The hair is softer then and is easier to shave. The best way to shave is to use an electric razor. Electric razors are made so that they can't cut you and are therefore a lot safer than regular razors. Some electric razors use batteries and don't need to be plugged into an outlet. Others have a cord that you plug in.

Another way to get rid of hair from legs or armpits is to use a hair removal cream. Hair removal cream can be bought at a drug store or pharmacy. It is easy to use. You just squeeze out some cream and spread it on your legs or on your underarms, wait a few minutes, then wipe it off with a wet cloth. The hair comes off and is wiped away. Be sure to carefully read the directions that come with the hair removal cream.

Using hair removal cream takes longer than shaving, because you have to wait before you wipe the cream off. Shaving with an electric razor is probably the easiest way to get rid of unwanted hair.

Some girls shave every day, some shave a couple of times a week. When it's warm and you're wearing shorts or a sleeveless shirt, you will probably want to shave or use hair removal cream more often. Just keep checking your legs and underarms and see how often you need to shave to keep from looking hairy. Once you've figured this out, add shaving to your hygiene checklist on those days.

Put on deodorant after you shave your underarms. If you put the deodorant on before you shave, you will just shave the deodorant off. If you shave your legs, rub a little lotion on them afterwards to keep them from feeling dry.

Things to remember about shaving:

1. Shave regularly

2. Put deodorant on after you shave

1. Shave regularly

2. Put lotion on after you shave

? Questions

✓ Tick all answers that are correct.

1.   When is the best time to shave?

    ☐ After you put deodorant on

    ☐ After your bath or shower

    ☐ Before you put deodorant on

2.   What happens if you put deodorant on before you shave?

    ☐ Your razor won't work

    ☐ You shave off the deodorant

    ☐ You could start smelling bad because you don't have any deodorant on

3.   How do you use hair removal cream?

    ☐ You rub it on, wait, then wipe it off

    ☐ You use it in the shower

    ☐ You rub it on and shave it off with a razor

List the 3 things you need to remember about shaving your underarms and legs.

1.   _____

2.   _____

3.   _____

7. Putting Your Best Foot Forward

Words to know:

Bacteria – tiny living things that can be seen only through a microscope. Bacteria are everywhere. Some bacteria are very useful and other bacteria cause people to get sick

Nail clippers – a small tool used to clip fingernails and toenails

Perspiring – another word for sweating

We all like to make a good impression, whether we're at school, having fun with friends, or working at a job. Trying to make a good impression by looking good is what is meant by the saying "putting your best foot forward."

But it's hard to make a good impression if your feet stink. The feet are another part of the body that perspires a lot and can smell bad if they aren't kept clean.

The most important thing to do to keep your feet smelling good is to remember to wash them with soap when you take your daily shower or bath.

Rinse all the soap off and dry them well with a towel, making sure to dry between your toes.

After your bath or shower is the best time to trim your toenails, because they are softer then. Toenails need to be trimmed once a week because long toenails collect dirt and bacteria under them and they can poke holes in your socks. Use a nail clipper or small scissors to cut your toenails straight across, being careful not to cut them too short.

Socks start smelling bad because of the sweat and bacteria that get on them. That's why it's important to put on clean socks every day.

To keep your feet looking and smelling good:

1. Wash feet with soap

2. Dry feet well

3. Trim your toenails

4. Put on clean socks

? Questions

✓ Tick all answers that are correct.

1. Why is it important to keep your feet clean?

   ☐ Dirty feet look gross

   ☐ Feet perspire a lot and they can smell bad if you don't keep them clean

   ☐ Dirty feet can give you bad breath

2. When is the best time to trim your toenails?

   ☐ Before your bath or shower

   ☐ After your bath or shower

   ☐ Before going to the bathroom

3. How often do you need to trim your toenails?

   ☐ Once a day

   ☐ Twice a day

   ☐ Once a week

   ☐ Once a year on New Year's Eve

4. Why is it important to wear clean socks every day?

   ☐ Socks start smelling bad because of the sweat and bacteria they get on them

   ☐ So your feet don't stink

   ☐ So that there are plenty of dirty clothes to wash

List the 4 steps to keeping your feet looking and smelling clean.

I. _____

2. _____

3. _____

4. _____

8. Face Up to Teenage Skin

Words to know:

Acne – a skin condition that causes pimples on the face or upper body

Acne medication – cream or lotion that can be put on the skin to help make pimples go away

Dermatologist – a doctor who treats acne and other skin conditions

Non-acnegenic – means it will not cause acne

Pimple – a small swelling of the skin

Another thing that changes when we become teenagers is our skin. Most teenagers get some pimples on their face and sometimes on their neck, shoulders, chest, and back. When this happens, it is called acne.

Acne happens because during the teenage years the oil glands in the skin make extra oil. This oil can mix with dead skin cells and block the openings in the skin that are called pores. When the pores get blocked, they swell up and make a pimple. Some people call these "zits."

Almost all teenagers get some pimples. It's just part of being a teenager, but there are things you can do to help your skin to look good.

Every morning and night wash your face with warm water and soap. When you wash your face, rub it very gently with your hands. Rubbing hard can actually make your skin look worse. Rinse well by letting water run over your face in the shower or splash water on your face using your hands. Afterwards, pat your face gently with a towel to dry it. Don't rub.

One of the times you wash your face will be when you take your daily bath or shower. If you bathe in the morning, you will also need to wash your face before you go to bed. If you bathe at night, wash your face after you get up in the morning.

Washing your face twice a day is important to wash away the extra oil and the dead skin cells so they don't block the pores and cause pimples.

After you wash your face, if you have any pimples, it's a good idea to use an acne cleansing pad or put on some acne medication or acne cream. You can buy these at a drugstore or supermarket. It's important to carefully follow the directions that come with the acne cleansing pads or acne medication. Don't use more than it says or it can dry your skin out and make it look worse.

It's also important to make sure that things that touch your skin are clean – things like your hair, eyeglasses if you wear them, and the pillowcase on your pillow. Keeping your skin looking good is another reason to shampoo your hair every day. If you wear glasses, wash them every day. Put a clean pillowcase on your pillow at least once a week.

Remember too that your hands have oil and dirt on them, so try to remember not to touch your face. And never squeeze or try to pop a pimple. This can hurt your skin and make it look red and puffy. People also think that it looks really gross to see someone picking at a pimple.

Girls who wear make-up should look for the words "oil-free" or "non-acnegenic" on the jar or package of face powder or liquid make-up. If it doesn't say "oil-free" or "non-acnegenic," it probably has oil in it which can block your pores and cause pimples.

If you still have lots of pimples even though you are taking good care of your skin, talk to your parents about going to see a doctor. There are special doctors called dermatologists who can help get rid of acne and scars on the skin that are left by pimples.

The 3 important steps for good-looking skin are:

1. Gently wash your face every morning and night

2. Use acne medication if needed

3. Never squeeze a pimple

? Questions

✓ **Tick all answers that are correct.**

1. What causes pimples?

   ☐ Washing your face

   ☐ Pores that get blocked with oil and dead skin cells

   ☐ Drinking lots of water

2. What should you do to keep your skin looking good?

   ☐ Gently wash your face morning and night

   ☐ Scrub your face hard with a washcloth every night

   ☐ Try not to touch your face

3. Why is it important not to squeeze a pimple?

   ☐ It can hurt your skin

   ☐ It can make your skin look worse

   ☐ People think it looks gross when they see someone squeezing a pimple

4. Why is it important to shampoo your hair every day?

   ☐ So your hair will look and smell clean

   ☐ So you don't get holes in your socks

   ☐ To help prevent pimples

5. What can happen if you use too much acne medication?

    ☐ It can make your hair look oily

    ☐ It will clear up all your pimples extra fast

    ☐ It can make your skin look worse

List the 3 steps to having good looking skin.

1. _____

2. _____

3. _____

9. Good Bathroom Hygiene

Words to know:

Bathroom hygiene – using good habits to keep clean and healthy when using the bathroom

Bathroom stall – the enclosed area with a toilet in a restroom

Bowel movement – when solid waste material comes out of the body

Penis – the male sex organ, which also has an opening for urine to leave the body

Urinal – a device to urinate in, found on the walls in men's restrooms

Urinating – when the yellow liquid waste material called urine comes out of the body

---

Boys

Everyone uses the toilet throughout the day. People urinate or go pee many times during the day and have a bowel movement or poop once a day or every other day. When we urinate or have a bowel movement our bodies are getting rid of wastes, which our bodies don't need. These wastes are full of bacteria which smell bad and can make us sick if they get back into our bodies. That's why it's important to practice good bathroom hygiene, so the bacteria in our wastes don't end up making us sick.

It's also important to practice good bathroom hygiene so that pee or poop doesn't end up on our hands or clothes, which can make us smell really bad. Often we won't notice the smell because we have become used to it, but other people will smell it and think it smells really bad.

The first thing to do to have good bathroom hygiene is to be careful when you urinate that the urine goes into the toilet or urinal and does not get on your hands or clothes. After finishing urinating, gently shake your penis to shake off the last few drops of urine.

After having a bowel movement, measure out about 6 to 8 squares of toilet paper and fold it. Carefully wipe away any poop then throw the toilet paper in the toilet.

It's very important to wash your hands with soap and water each time after you urinate or have a bowel movement. Washing gets rid of the bacteria that might have gotten onto your hands. If you don't get rid of any bacteria, it could make you sick and it could make your hands smell bad.

Also, make sure you wash your groin area well when you take your daily bath or shower. That way you will wash away any urine or poop that might not have been wiped away when you used the toilet.

Often we need to use a public restroom, when we are at school, at a restaurant or shopping center, etc. Public restrooms are a little different because usually they have urinals. Men and boys stand in front of urinals and use them when they urinate. When standing at a urinal, a boy unzips his pants and pulls out his penis to urinate. If a boy is wearing pants that don't open in front, like sweat pants, then he just pulls the pants down in front

far enough to get his penis out. When using a public restroom, it is best to try to choose a urinal that is not right next to one that is being used. Also, when in a public restroom, boys and men don't usually look at each other or talk to each other.

When you need to have a bowel movement in a public restroom, then go into a stall with a toilet, close the door and use the toilet as you would at home. It's even more important to remember to wash your hands after using a public restroom, because it may not be as clean as your home bathroom.

The important things to remember for good bathroom hygiene are:

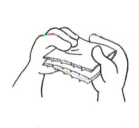

1. Be careful not to get urine on your hands or clothes	**2. Use toilet paper to wipe after a bowel movement**	**3. Wash your hands after going to the bathroom**

? Questions

✓ **Tick all answers that are correct.**

1. What can happen if you don't have good bathroom hygiene?

    ☐ People can smell the urine or poop

    ☐ You could get sick

    ☐ You might get dandruff

2. What do you need to do every time you go to the bathroom?

    ☐ Use a urinal

    ☐ Use toilet paper

    ☐ Wash your hands afterwards

3. About how much toilet paper do you need to wipe yourself after a bowel movement?

    ☐ About 6 to 8 squares

    ☐ I square

    ☐ About 20 squares

4. Which of the following do boys and men do in a public restroom?

    ☐ Try to use a urinal that is away from ones that are being used

    ☐ Always say "Hi" to everyone that comes in

    ☐ Close the door when using a bathroom stall

    ☐ Look at other boys who are using the urinal

    ☐ Talk to other boys who are using the urinal

List the 3 things you need to do to have good bathroom hygiene.

1. _____

2. _____

3. _____

Girls

Words to know:

Bathroom hygiene – using good habits to keep clean and healthy when using the bathroom

Bowel movement – when solid waste material comes out of the body

Feminine hygiene – using good habits to keep clean and healthy when menstruating

Infection – an unhealthy condition caused by bacteria

Menstruation – when blood flows through the vagina and out of the body

Sanitary napkins – soft cotton pads that are placed inside underpants to absorb blood during menstruation

Tampons – absorbent cotton, shaped like a tube of lipstick, which is placed inside the vagina to absorb blood during menstruation

Urinating – when the yellow liquid waste material called urine comes out of the body

Vagina – an opening that is part of the female sex organs. Blood flows out of the vagina during menstruation.

Everyone uses the toilet throughout the day. People urinate or go pee many times during the day and have a bowel movement or poop once a day or every other day. When we urinate or have a bowel movement our bodies are getting rid of wastes, which our bodies don't need. These wastes are full of bacteria which smell bad and can make us sick if they get back into our bodies. That's why it's important to practice good bathroom hygiene, so the bacteria in our wastes don't end up making us sick.

It's also important to practice good bathroom hygiene so that pee or poop doesn't end up on our hands or clothes, which can make us smell really bad. Often we won't notice the smell because we have become used to it, but other people will smell it and think it smells really bad.

To avoid getting urine on your clothes, make sure that you pull your pants down far enough so they are away from the toilet. If you are wearing a dress or skirt, make sure to hold it up out of the way. To avoid getting pee or poop on your hands, make sure you use enough toilet paper whenever you urinate or have a bowel movement. Measure out about 6 to 8 squares of toilet paper and fold them into a square. Wipe yourself from front to back. If you don't wipe from front to back, you could get an infection which can make your groin area itch and sting. It can also make you very sick.

It's very important to wash your hands with soap and water each time after you urinate or have a bowel movement. Washing gets rid of the bacteria that might have gotten onto your hands. If you don't get rid of any bacteria, it could make you sick and it could make your hands smell bad.

Also, make sure you wash your groin area well when you take your daily bath or shower. That way you will wash away any urine or poop that might not have been wiped away when you used the toilet.

The important things for girls to remember about bathroom hygiene are:

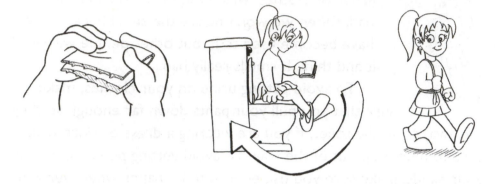

1. Measure out enough toilet paper

2. Wipe from front to back

3. Wash your hands

Girls and women also need to make sure they have good feminine hygiene. This means that they look and smell clean when they are menstruating. Girls begin menstruating usually somewhere between the ages of 11 and 14, though it can be earlier or later than that. During menstruation blood flows out of the vagina, between your legs. This is normal. It's the body's way of getting ready to be able to have children. Menstruation, or some people call it "your period," happens about once a month and can last for just two or three days, or it may last as long as seven or eight days.

Since blood is flowing out of your vagina, you will need something to soak up the blood so it doesn't get on your clothes. When most girls first start having their period, they use sanitary napkins or pads. These are easy to use. The pad has a plastic covering on the bottom with a strip of paper stuck to it. When you pull off this paper, it's sticky underneath. Place the sticky part inside your underpants.

There are lots of different kinds of pads. There are ones that are thin, for when there isn't much blood coming out of you. When not much blood is coming out, you say your flow is light. These thin ones have words on the box like "mini," "light," and "slender." There are really thick pads for when your flow is heavy or a lot of blood is coming out of you. These are also good to wear at night while you are sleeping. These have words on the box like "super," "maxi," and "absorbent." Then there are "regular" pads that are not real thin and not real thick for when your flow isn't really heavy and isn't really light, but is somewhere in between.

Some girls like to use tampons instead of pads. Tampons go up inside you in your vagina, so if you want to go swimming you can. You can't go swimming while you are wearing a pad. But since a tampon has to be put in the vagina, it's a little harder to use and you can't really tell when you need to change it. So when a girl starts having her periods, it's easier to use pads.

What's important so that you look and smell clean during your period, is to change your pad every three to four hours, except when you're sleeping. This is important even if it doesn't have that much blood on it. A pad will start smelling after three or four hours even if there's hardly any blood on it.

The best place to change your pad is sitting on the toilet. This means you will need to carry extra pads with you in your purse or backpack or someplace that no one will see them. Sanitary napkins or pads are private things that you keep put away until you get inside the restroom.

To change your pad, pull off the dirty pad and wrap it in toilet paper. Then put a clean pad in your underpants. You should never throw the dirty pad in the toilet. It will stop up the toilet. Instead throw it in a trash container. Afterwards, wash your hands with soap and water.

If you write down on a calendar or chart (ask your doctor for one) when you have your period, then you will know about when it will be time for your period to start next time. This is a really good idea so that you'll be watching for it and have a pad with you. It can be embarrassing if you start your period and get blood on your clothes. If you don't have a pad with you, you can always fold up some toilet paper and put it in your underpants until you can get a pad. If you get caught without a pad, ask your mother or a friend or teacher for help.

The important things for girls to remember about feminine hygiene are:

| 1. Change your pad every three or four hours | 2. Wrap the dirty pad in toilet paper and throw it in the trash | 3. Wash your hands |

? Questions

✓ **Tick all answers that are correct.**

1. Why is good bathroom hygiene important?

   ☐ So you don't smell bad

   ☐ To help you stay healthy

   ☐ Good bathroom hygiene isn't important

2. What can happen if you don't wipe from the front to the back?

   ☐ You'll run out of toilet paper

   ☐ You'll start your period

   ☐ You could get an infection

3. When do you need to wash your hands?

   ☐ After you use the toilet

   ☐ After you take a shower

   ☐ Before you eat

   ☐ After you change your sanitary napkin

4. How often should you change your sanitary napkin?

   ☐ Every half hour

   ☐ Once a day

   ☐ Every three to four hours

   ☐ In the morning and again at night

5. Why is it important to change your pad even if it doesn't have that much blood on it?

☐ Because it will start to smell bad

☐ Because you can't throw it in the toilet

☐ So you will need to buy more pads

List the 3 things you need to do to have good bathroom hygiene.

1. _____

2. _____

3. _____

List the 3 things you need to do to have good feminine hygiene.

1. _____

2. _____

3. _____

Supplementary Material

Final Quiz

✓ **Tick all answers that are correct.**

Why is having good personal hygiene important?

☐ So you will smell good

☐ So you will stay healthy

☐ So you will look clean

When do you need to put deodorant on?

☐ Every day after your bath or shower

☐ 2 or 3 times a week

☐ When you feel yourself sweating

Which parts of the body perspire the most?

☐ Underarms, hands and neck

☐ Groin area, feet and elbows

☐ Underarms, groin area, and feet

How often do you need to take a shower or bath?

    ☐ Whenever you think that you smell bad

    ☐ Once a day

    ☐ Twice a week

What do you need to do so that you don't have bad breath?

    ☐ Brush your teeth every morning and every night

    ☐ Brush your tongue every time you brush your teeth

    ☐ Drink lots of coffee

Which of the following do you need to do once every day?

    ☐ Take a bath or shower

    ☐ Use deodorant

    ☐ Trim your toenails

When do you need to wash your hands?

    ☐ After going to the bathroom

    ☐ Before eating or touching food

    ☐ After cleaning your room

What happens to hair if you don't shampoo regularly?

    ☐ It all falls out

    ☐ It looks oily

    ☐ It smells bad

When brushing your teeth, how long do you need to brush?

    ☐ 30 seconds

    ☐ 10 minutes

    ☐ 2 minutes

How often do you need to floss your teeth?

☐ Whenever you see food stuck between your teeth

☐ 2 or 3 times a week

☐ Once a day

Activity Pages 1–10

Using the activity pages

The ten activity pages are designed to accompany the different lessons presented. The descriptions below list which topics are covered in each activity and after which lesson it may be used.

Activity Page 1

- ○ Daily bathing and using deodorant
- ○ Use anytime after presenting "Looking Clean, Smelling Clean"

Activity Page 2

- ○ Daily bathing and hair care
- ○ Use anytime after presenting "Turning Bad Hair Days into Good Hair Days"

Activity Page 3

- ○ Daily bathing, hair care, and dental hygiene
- ○ Use anytime after presenting "Clean Teeth, Great Smile"

Activity Page 4

- ○ Bathing, using deodorant, hair care, dental hygiene, and bad breath
- ○ Use anytime after presenting "Taming Dragon Breath"

Activity Page 5

- ○ Hand washing
- ○ Use anytime after presenting "Having a Hand People Want to Shake"

Activity Page 6

- ○ Unwanted hair
- ○ Use anytime after presenting "There's Hair Everywhere"

Activity Page 7

- ○ Foot care
- ○ Use anytime after presenting "Putting Your Best Foot Forward"

Activity Page 8

- ○ Facial care
- ○ Use anytime after presenting "Face Up to Teenage Skin"

Activity Page 9 (Boys)

- ○ Bathroom hygiene for boys
- ○ Use anytime after presenting "Good Bathroom Hygiene"

Activity Page 9 (Girls)

- ○ Menstruation and feminine hygiene
- ○ Use anytime after presenting "Good Bathroom Hygiene"

Activity Page 1: Looking Clean Crossword Puzzle

Use the words from the word bank to work out the crossword puzzle.

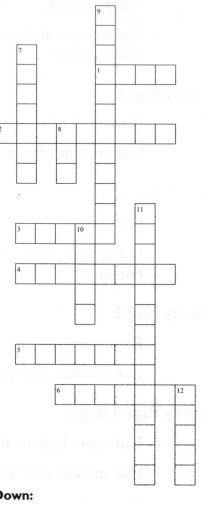

Word Bank

after	deodorant
antiperspirant	hygiene
armpits	nervous
bacteria	perspiration
clean	smell
day	soap

Across:

1. Use _____ every day when you take a bath or shower.

2. Use _____ every day after your bath or shower.

3. After bathing, put on _____ clothes.

4. _____ are too small to see, but they can make you sick.

5. We sweat more when we are _____.

6. When bathing, wash the _____ and groin areas well.

Down:

7. _____ is the practice of keeping yourself clean.

8. It's important to take a bath or shower every _____.

9. A bath or shower washes away _____.

10. Put deodorant on _____ you bathe.

11. _____ goes under your arms to prevent perspiration.

12. It's important to bathe every day, so that you don't _____.

Activity Page 2: Good Hygiene Maze

Help our dirty friend find his way through the maze to good personal hygiene.

Activity Page 3: Hygiene Word Search

Find and circle all the words from the word bank in the puzzle below.

Word bank

antiperspirant

bath

deodorant

floss

hygiene

shampoo

shower

soap

toothbrush

toothpaste

a	d	s	o	a	p	o	i	s	r	n	g	e
n	e	h	o	s	r	s	h	t	t	o	o	a
t	o	o	t	h	b	r	u	s	h	e	o	o
i	d	w	a	a	i	e	s	y	y	i	o	p
p	o	e	r	m	h	n	t	t	g	a	r	o
e	r	r	o	p	e	w	a	t	i	s	h	s
r	a	f	l	o	s	s	t	b	e	i	t	h
s	n	b	m	o	o	r	s	i	n	m	h	a
p	t	h	a	i	t	e	o	t	e	a	a	p
i	f	g	t	b	e	e	b	a	o	r	y	s
r	s	o	o	b	n	i	t	a	t	e	o	e
a	o	o	h	a	t	p	m	e	f	s	o	h
n	e	r	o	t	h	t	e	t	t	t	s	
t	o	o	t	h	p	a	s	t	e	p	o	h

Activity Page 4: Mind Reading

Draw a line to match each caption with the correct cartoon or make up your own captions.

"That is so gross! It looks like he's got bugs crawling around in his teeth."

"I'm going to gag! This guy is so dirty and his hair is all over the place. Hasn't he ever heard of shampoo?"

"I can't stand it! His breath is so bad that it makes my eyes water. When was the last time he brushed his teeth?"

"P.U.! Does this guy stink or what? This couch needs to be a whole lot longer to get away from the smell."

Activity Page 5: Hand Washing Secret Code

Change each letter to the letter that comes before it in the alphabet in order to find out important times to wash your hands.

bgufs vtjoh uif upjmfu

___ ___ ___ ___

cfgpsf fbujoh

___ ___

cfgpsf upvdijoh gppe

___ ___ ___

bgufs iboemjoh hbscbhf

___ ___ ___

Activity 6 (Boys): Hidden Message

Start with the upper left hand circle and follow the arrows to figure out the hidden message below.

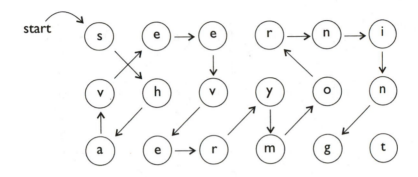

start

S _ _ _ _ _   _ _ _ _ _ _

_ _ _ _ _ _

Activity 6 (Girls): Hidden Message

Start with the upper left hand circle and follow the arrows to figure out the hidden message below.

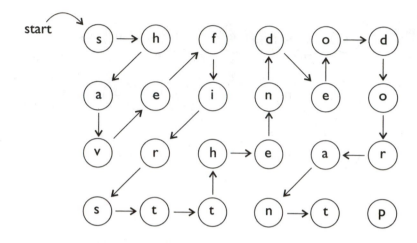

start

S h a v e   f i r s t ,   t h e n

d e o d o r a n t

Activity Page 7: Foot Care Word Switch

Read the first paragraph. Then switch around the bold words and write them in the second paragraph, so it makes sense.

Keep your **socks** looking and smelling good by washing them with **feet** every day, drying them well and putting on clean **toenails**. When drying your **soap**, dry between your **nail clippers**. Trim your **feet** with a pair of **toes** or small scissors.

Keep your _____ looking and smelling good by washing them with _____ every day, drying them well and putting on clean _____. When drying your _____, dry between your _____. Trim your _____ with a pair of _____ or small scissors.

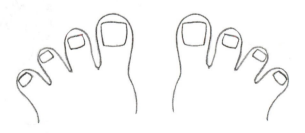

Activity Page 8: Taking Care of Your Face

Use the secret code to figure and the message below.

a	b	c	d	e	f	g	h	i	j	k	l	m
§	♥	?	∞	<	¬	ø	=	^	μ	}	#	ð

n	o	p	q	r	s	t	u	v	w	x	y	z
+	~	Ÿ	>	‡	¢	Þ	Υ	@	*	ƒ	$	¶

* § ¢ = $ ~ Υ ‡   ¬ § ? <

_ _ _ _   _ _ _ _   _ _ _ _

ð ~ ‡ + ^ + ø   § + ∞

_ _ _ _ _ _ _   _ _ _

+ ^ ø = Þ

_ _ _ _ _

Activity 9 (Boys): Bathroom Word Scramble

Use the word bank to help unscramble the words.

eunir — — — — —

ottlei reppa — — — — — —　— — — — — —

lobew veetommn — — — — —　— — — — — —

sinep — — — — —

homabtor geenihy — — — — — — — —　— — — — — — —

cietabar — — — — — — —

natiuer — — — — — — —

meosorrt — — — — — — — —

arnuil — — — — — —

moobarth lalst — — — — — — — —　— — — — —

Word bank

toilet paper

bowel movement

urinal

bathroom hygiene　　urinate　　bathroom stall

penis

urine　　bacteria

rest room

Activity Page 9 (Girls): Time to Change?

Circle the right answer in each row

You changed your pad at...	You need to change your pad again by...		
7:00a.m.	8.00a.m.	11:00a.m.	2:00p.m.
2:30p.m.	4:00p.m.	12:00a.m.	6:30p.m.
5:00p.m.	9:00p.m.	9:00a.m.	10:00p.m.
8:30a.m.	10:30a.m.	3:30p.m.	12:30p.m.
10:00p.m.	When you get up in the morning	2:00a.m.	12:00p.m.
11:45a.m.	1:45p.m.	3:45p.m.	5:45p.m.

See for Yourself Activities

The following are hands-on activities that can be used to demonstrate some of the key points that are made throughout the book.

Using deodorant

To demonstrate how deodorant and antiperspirant protect against odor, cut an absorbent paper towel in half and on each half use a marker to draw a small circle approximately 3 inches in diameter. Rub deodorant or antiperspirant all over the circle on one of the paper towels. Put nothing on the other paper towel. Next take a slice of onion or a clove of garlic and rub it inside the circles on both paper towels. Then smell the paper towels. You should be able to smell the onion on the paper towel that does not have deodorant on it and not smell it on the paper towel treated with deodorant.

Using shampoo

To demonstrate why shampoo is needed to get the hair clean, you will need two wigs or two doll heads with hair. If these are not available, yarn or pieces of fabric can be gathered together with a rubber band. Spray the wigs with nonstick vegetable spray to show the oil that naturally gets on hair from oil glands. Wash the first wig with water only. Wash the second wig using shampoo and rinse thoroughly. Dry wigs with a hair dryer or allow to air dry. Compare the two wigs.

The wigs can also be used to demonstrate the importance of not using too much shampoo and of rinsing thoroughly. Shampoo one wig with an excessive amount of shampoo and rinse quickly, not removing all the shampoo.

Brushing teeth

To demonstrate the correct way to brush teeth, use a set of wax or plastic teeth purchased at a party store. Other sets could be used for students to practice on.

To demonstrate the amount of time that should be spent brushing teeth, give everyone a toothbrush and a cup of water. Set a timer for 2 minutes and have everyone brush their teeth with water until the timer goes off.

Bad breath

Students can check their own breath using the following methods.

- ○ Have students wipe the top surface of their tongue with a small piece of cotton gauze and then smell it. A yellowish stain on the gauze can also indicate the likelihood of bad breath.

- ○ Have students use a piece of unflavored dental floss and floss between some of their back teeth, then smell the floss.

- ○ Use a small mirror, or other small round object, and have the student hold it by their mouth and breathe on it through their mouth.

Breath monitors that provide a digital visual indication of bad breath can also be purchased.

Hand care

To demonstrate the importance of hand washing, spray cooking spray on students' hands and sprinkle on some cinnamon or paprika to simulate germs. Have students observe how easily the "germs" transfer from one surface to another. Have students compare the difference between unwashed hands, hands washed quickly, hands washed with only water and hands washed with soap and water for 20 seconds.

Another way to demonstrate how easily germs are spread is to cover a pencil with glue, then sprinkle glitter all over the glue. Pass the pencil around and see how the glittering "germs" pass from one student to another.

To demonstrate the correct way to clean and trim nails, bring in nail brushes, nail files, and clippers. Show the students how to use these and let students try them out.

Shaving

Bring in an electric razor for demonstration.

Facial skin care

Using a small dishpan of water, have each student wash his or her face. An alternative would be to use large dolls or doll heads to demonstrate face washing. Splash water on face, lather with a mild soap, using hands or a soft washcloth. Emphasize gentle rubbing. Splash water on to rinse and pat dry.

To demonstrate the importance of using soap and water to remove excess oil, provide each student with a section of plastic canvas, approximately 2 inches by 4 inches. (Plastic canvases can be purchased at art and craft stores. They are the backing that is used in doing needlepoint.) Use a waterproof marker to draw a line dividing each section into halves. Tell students that the plastic canvas is like their skin, with lots of tiny holes or pores.

Have students mix together equal parts of cooking oil (to represent the oil in their skin) and flour (to represent dead skin cells). A teaspoon of each (oil and flour) is usually sufficient. Ask students to spread the oily mix over their plastic canvas. Note how the mixture blocks the holes or pores. Next have students rinse one side with a little cool water. Note that it clears away some of the oily mixture, but much of it is left. Next have students gently wash the other side of the plastic canvas with soap and warm water, then rinse. Washing with soap and water gets rid of most of the oily mixture.

Bathroom hygiene

Bring in rolls of toilet paper. Have students practice measuring out an appropriate amount of toilet paper and folding it.

For girls

Bring in a baby doll. Demonstrate with the doll how to wipe from front to back. Have girls practice wiping the doll's bottom.

Bring in a variety of different types of sanitary napkins to show the difference in sizes and how some have "wings" and some don't. Also bring in underpants and demonstrate how a pad is placed on a pair of underpants. Have girls practice placing the pads onto underpants.

Provide each girl with a sanitary napkin and some toilet paper. Put a few drops of red food coloring on each sanitary napkin and have girls wrap the pad in toilet paper and throw it in the trash. Discuss what will happen if the pad is thrown in the toilet.

Personal Stories

Using the personal stories

The following pages include text for four personal stories which can accompany the hygiene lessons. They cover the areas of bathing, using deodorant, hair care, and hand washing. These stories are similar to the social stories that Carol Gray describes in *The New Social Story Book: Illustrated Edition* (2000) and in subsequent books. The idea of these personal stories, and of social stories in general, is to provide the student with relevant social information (including how others view the situation) and to define appropriate actions or responses.

The stories as presented here are very general, but can be individualized by adding personal details to the text. The more personalized a story is, the more relevant it will be for the student. Stories can also be made more meaningful by adding pictures. Clip-art, picture symbols or photographs can be added, or students can illustrate their own stories by drawing pictures or cutting and gluing relevant pictures from magazines.

The stories are written in the first person, to be read by the student. For students who cannot read fluently, the stories can be read to them or put on audio cassette tapes. How often the stories are used depends on the student, but stories are most effective when reviewed on a regular basis until they are no longer needed. Further details and ideas for use can be found in *The New Social Story Book: Illustrated Edition* by (2000) Carol Gray.

1. Keeping clean

Now that I'm a teenager, I sweat more, particularly my underarms. When my underarms sweat, they can make a bad odor. This bad odor gets on my clothes and makes my clothes smell bad.

Usually I can't smell the odor because my nose has gotten used to it and I don't notice it. But other people smell the odor and they think it stinks. People don't like to smell stinky body odor.

There are things I can do to make sure that I don't smell bad.

- I can take a bath or shower every day and wash all over with soap, particularly under my arms. That will wash the sweat off.

- After my bath or shower, I can put on deodorant. That will keep my underarms from smelling bad.

- Then I can put on clean clothes.

Every day I will try to take a bath or shower, use deodorant and put on clean clothes. Then I will look and smell clean. Other people like it when I look and smell clean.

2. Clean hair

Now that I'm a teenager, my hair glands produce more oil, which will make my hair look dirty and oily. The dirt and oil can make my hair smell bad too. If I want to keep my hair looking good, I need to shampoo more often than when I was younger.

I may not notice that my hair looks oily and messy because I only see it when I look in a mirror. I probably can't smell when my hair stinks because my nose has gotten used to the smell. But other people are looking at my hair all the time. They will notice if my hair looks oily and dirty. They will notice if my hair smells bad. People think oily, stinky hair is gross. They don't like it.

There are things I can do to make sure that my hair looks and smells clean and neat.

- ○ I can shampoo my hair every day when I take a bath or shower.

- ○ I can dry and comb my hair after I shampoo it.

Every day I will try to shampoo and comb my hair. Then my hair will look and smell clean. Other people will be glad that my hair looks clean and neat.

3. Clean teeth, good smelling breath

When I eat, food gets all over my teeth and stuck between my teeth. If the food particles are not washed away, they make my teeth look dirty and yellow and can cause cavities.

I can't tell that my teeth are dirty unless I look at them closely in a mirror. But other people see my teeth whenever I talk or smile. They notice when my teeth are dirty and they think dirty teeth look disgusting.

Inside my mouth is dark and wet and lots of bacteria grow there. They grow on my teeth, between my teeth, and on my tongue. Bacteria make my breath stink.

I can't smell when my breath smells bad because my nose is used to the smell, but other people smell my breath whenever I talk or laugh. They notice when my breath smells bad. People do not like to smell bad breath. They will turn their head or back away.

There are things I can do to make sure that my teeth look clean and my breath smells good.

- ○ I can brush my teeth twice a day, in the morning and at night.

- ○ After I brush my teeth, I can brush my tongue with my toothbrush.

Every day I will try to brush my teeth in the morning and at night. I will also try to remember to brush my tongue every time I brush my teeth. Then my teeth will look clean and my breath will smell good.

4. Clean hands

It is important to wash my hands often. I can't see germs, but they are everywhere and I get them on my hands from things that I touch. Some germs can make me get sick with colds or the flu.

It's easy to forget to look at my hands to see if they look dirty. But since I'm always using my hands, other people see my hands and notice if they look dirty. People think dirty hands and dirty fingernails look gross. They don't want to touch things that I have touched with dirty hands. People will also notice if my fingernails are long or jagged. People think long, jagged fingernails look bad.

Even when my hands look clean, they can still have lots of germs on them that can make me sick. That is why it is important to wash my hands even when they don't look dirty.

There are things I can do to make sure that my hands are clean.

- I can wash my hands with soap and water before touching food, after using the toilet, and whenever I touch things that are dirty.

- I can clean my fingernails with a nailbrush or nail file.

- I can trim my fingernails with clippers or with a nail file.

I will try to remember to wash my hands every time before I eat and after I use the toilet. I will also try to keep my nails clean and trimmed. Then when other people see my hands they will be glad that my hands look clean and neat.

Having a Plan

Good Hygiene and Getting to School on Time

Now comes the hard part – actually doing all the things you need to do every day to have good hygiene. Part of having good hygiene is realizing that all these things like taking a shower, brushing your teeth and shampooing your hair are just things you have to do, even though you don't feel like doing them. Most people are sleepy and don't want to get up in the morning and they really don't want to get up extra early to shower and shampoo. Most people get busy or tired at night and don't want to take the time to shower before they go to bed. I don't know anyone that gets excited and yells "Hooray!" when it's time to shampoo or trim his toenails. But we have to do these things to keep healthy and so that other people won't think we smell or look dirty.

So now what you need is a plan. The first part of the plan is to decide whether you will do these hygiene tasks in the morning or in the evening. Below there is a list of all the things you need to do every day. Your nails only need to be trimmed or filed once a week and there are also some hygiene tasks that are optional, meaning that some people will want to add them to their checklists and other people won't.

After you've decided which tasks you are going to do every morning write an "M" next to them. The write an "E" next to the ones you are going to do in the evening. Follow the directions on the Personal Hygiene Worksheets 1, 2, and 3 to come up with your own personal plan for including hygiene as part of your day. Once it's all figured out, fill out a Hygiene Checklist or maybe two, one for the morning and one for the evening. And most important, take it home and use it!

Hygiene Tasks – To do every day

- Shower or bath using soap
- Shampoo hair
- Put on antiperspirant
- Comb hair
- Put on clean clothes
- Brush teeth – morning
- Brush teeth – evening
- Floss teeth
- Clean nails

Hygiene Tasks – To be done once a week

- Trim or file nails

Optional Hygiene Tasks

- Dry hair with hair dryer
- Curl hair
- Shave face
- Shave underarms or legs

Personal Hygiene Worksheets and Checklist

Personal Hygiene Worksheet 1

1.   List all the hygiene tasks you do in the morning under **Morning**.

2.   List everything else you do in the morning between getting up and leaving for school, e.g. eating breakfast, fixing lunch, watching TV.

3.   List all the hygiene tasks you do in the evening under **Evening**.

Morning	Evening

Personal Hygiene Worksheet 2

1. Under **Morning** list all the tasks you have to do in the morning in order.

2. Under **How many minutes?** write how much time it takes to do each task.

3. Starting with the time you need to leave for school, work backwards to figure out what time you need to get up. Write the times under **Time**.

Morning	How many minutes?	Time
Get up		
Leave for school		

Personal Hygiene Worksheet 3

1. Under **Evening** list all the tasks you have to do in the evening in order.

2. Under **How many minutes?** write how much time it takes to do each task.

3. Starting with the time you need to go to bed, work backwards to figure out what time you need to start. Write the times under **Time**.

Evening	How many minutes?	Time
Start doing hygiene		
Go to bed		

Hygiene Checklist

1. Write down all the hygiene tasks you need to do.

2. Write down the times you should begin doing these.

3. Check off tasks that you did.

Time	Tasks	Sun	Mon	Tues	Wed	Thur	Fri	Sat